SPIRITUAL MESSAGES
from

JAMES
ALLEN

THE TRUE MEANING OF
HAPPINESS AND SUCCESS

RYUHO OKAWA

HS PRESS

Contents

Preface 5

Spiritual Messages from James Allen
The true meaning of happiness and success

Preface

His words had a profound effect on me.

It came from the sound of silence.

It was an indistinct voice from the universe.

Now, here, he is. James Allen. My good old friend.

He has no body. He is the words.

He really is a holy voice.

He said "Now is the day of daylight of God."

And "So, now is your time to work."

Read these words again and again.

Picture Buddha and Jesus to yourself.

And visualize your Grand Master.

Ryuho Okawa
Founder & CEO of Happy Science Group
Nov. 21, 2017

Spiritual Messages from James Allen

The true meaning of happiness and success

Recorded March 25, 2014
Happy Science General Headquarters,
Japan

James Allen (1864~1912)

A British writer. At 15, he was forced to leave school after his father passed away, and later set off to study on his own as he worked. Enlightened by Tolstoy's works, Allen began his writing career at 38. He published *As a Man Thinketh* in 1903. He passed away at 48, after having produced a total of 19 works. *As a Man Thinketh*, his most famous book, had great influence on other self-help writers such as Dale Carnegie, Norman Vincent Peale and Napoleon Hill, and became the source of success philosophies in 20th century America. In Christian countries, the book is considered to be a longtime seller that comes second to the Bible. As a bible of self-help, it is still being read by people around the world.

Interviewers from Happy Science*:

Kazuhiro Ichikawa
Senior Managing Director
Chief Director of International Headquarters

Masashi Ishikawa
Deputy Chief Secretary, First Secretarial Division
Chief of Overseas Missionary Work Promotion Office
Religious Affairs Headquarters

Toshihisa Sakakibara
Executive Director
Director General of International Education and Training Division

*The opinions of the spirit do not necessarily
reflect those of Happy Science Group.*

* Interviewers are listed in the order that they appear in the transcript. Their
professional titles represent their positions at the time of the interview.

1

Thoughts of Allen that Inspired Many Successful Thought-Makers

RYUHO OKAWA

Today, we'd like to summon the famous James Allen, who lived about 100 years ago in England.

He inspired and influenced a lot of famous philosophers and successful thought-makers like Dale Carnegie, Norman Vincent Peale and Napoleon Hill. The feature of his thought is, he was very influenced by Buddhism, Christianity and other philosophies, and it sounded very original in Great Britain.

In Japan, his books have been published in these 20 years. It might be from the influence of Happy Science or my spiritual books. He wrote 19 books by the time he died at 48. He was born in 1864 and passed away in 1912, almost 100 years ago. His activity was very small, but his influence is becoming greater and greater.

And now, I'm thinking that our Happy Science philosophy will again prevail in Great Britain by dint of influence of James Allen. A lot of his thoughts were translated into Japanese and almost all of them were very similar to my philosophy of thinking, the power to control the mind and the way to remake life by thinking power. We can find a lot of similarities between James Allen's books and my books.

So, today, we have three great [*laughs*] English users and I guess they will succeed in approaching his philosophy. But he died 100 years ago in England, so his English might sometimes sound "dead." Nowadays we cannot understand such kind of English. And if he can understand your [Ishikawa's] fluent New York English and your [Sakakibara's] Filipino English*, I don't know exactly.

I'm afraid not, but OK. I can understand your Japanese, so please think in Japanese and I can translate it into his mind. And he can answer your question. OK? Then, we will try.

Good morning, famous James Allen.
Would you come down to
Happy Science General Headquarters?
I'll summon you.
Would you come down here
And give several messages and teachings
For the people who are seeking

---

* Ishikawa and Sakakibara both have experience as Happy Science branch manager in New York and Philippines respectively.

Spiritual enlightenment?

I want to convey the Buddhist-like Truth

Through your words to English people

And English-speaking people.

So, would you kindly help us

Spread our Truth all over the world?

James Allen, would you come down here, please?

[*About 13 seconds of silence.*]

2

Real Prosperity Lies in Your Mind

JAMES ALLEN

Ahh...

KAZUHIRO ICHIKAWA

Mr. James Allen?

ALLEN

Hmm.

ICHIKAWA

It's very much an honor to invite you here to Happy Science General Headquarters. We would like to ask you several questions about happiness and success. Is it OK to start interviewing you?

ALLEN

Before that, could you kindly teach me the main points of your grand principles of Happy Science?

ICHIKAWA

Actually... Yes. Our or Happy Science's main principle is the exploration of the Right Mind.

ALLEN

Exploring the Right Mind, OK.

ICHIKAWA

And the basic teachings are the same as those you taught in the world. It's like "good thoughts bear good fruit, bad thoughts bad fruit."

ALLEN

Good, good. Good words. Yes.

ICHIKAWA

It's what you said in your articles.

ALLEN

Good. A good tree bears good fruits. Yes. That's right. That's all. Bye-bye! [*Audience laughs.*]

ICHIKAWA

Those are the teachings you taught while you were on earth. Today, as you are in Heaven, certainly, so we would appreciate it if you could teach us further philosophy about happiness, success, prosperity and so on.

ALLEN

OK. My recognition about happiness and success is a little different from your recognitions.

I think, in my day, we, European people were apt to think that the reality of happiness lay in the materialistic world and materialistic prosperity. This was because of industrial development; people were seeking for greater prosperity through a lot of affluent goods and the food, money and fame which could be obtained through activities in human lives.

But I had quite the opposite thinking to these because I, like Jesus Christ said, wanted to say that your real prosperity lies in your own heart or your own mind.

People misunderstood this Truth. People were seeking materialistic prosperity only. So, I fought against this phenomenon of the affluent society. This is the meaning of "the cause and effect of the mind" and the spiritual rule, which I taught a lot in my books. Is this almost the same as your teachings? Can you understand? Understand?

ICHIKAWA

OK. Thank you very much.

ALLEN

Understand? You understand? Oh, really?

3

To Be Pure in Your Mind

MASASHI ISHIKAWA

In this world, both good and bad thoughts will eventually manifest, I think. But I think you emphasized the realization of selfless love. In your famous book, *As a Man Thinketh*...

ALLEN

Thin*keth* ([θiŋkiθ]). Thinketh.

ISHIKAWA

Yes. Sorry [*laughs*]. "The universe does not favor the greedy, the dishonest, or the vicious although on the mere surface it may sometimes appear to do so; it helps the honest, the noble and the good." So maybe we need to discern the good from the bad...

ALLEN

*Ho*nest. Honest. It's pronounced *aw*-nest ([ɔ́nəst]). OK?

ISHIKAWA

Honest. I'm so sorry about my poor English. So, yes. Why did you emphasize selfless love or the importance of selfless love?

ALLEN

It's just to *beautifly* [bjúːtɪflɑɪ] your life. Could you understand the word, "beautifly"? Not butterfly, *beautifly*.

ISHIKAWA

The beauty of our soul?

ALLEN

Yes. To make your life more beautiful. To be beautiful is to be pure in your mind. People don't know the importance of purifying their own minds. Could you explain the importance of purity in your heart? Why? Why is it important for you or for other people to purify their minds? Why?

ISHIKAWA

Maybe, I think, true success needs several conditions...

ALLEN

Conditions.

ISHIKAWA

...and maybe one of them is "love"? Maybe true success needs to be based on love.

ALLEN

Could you persuade modern people by your theory? Modern people seek love before success. Is that right?

ISHIKAWA

That's because, I think, now many people do not believe in the other world but only in this material world. Yes.

For example, I think that maybe you are the source of self-help movement. Recently, the famous book, *The Secret* by Rhonda Byrne became a worldwide bestseller and the law of attraction is well-known to modern people. But I think that the content is very superficial or shallow compared with your thoughts. I think that maybe your thoughts are based on true faith or...

ALLEN

That's bad. Bad book! It's a magician's book. It's a little different.

4

What is Important is the Foundation, Not Conditions

ISHIKAWA

I think that the mind is two-fold: we have surface consciousness and the subconscious. The subconscious can't discern good from bad, so automatically, our strong desires are realized.

But I think true self-realization needs some conditions because this world was created by God. If we deny God or deny faith, we can't persuade those materialistic people or non-religious people. In this world, sometimes religious people are not so successful and greedy people or people who have strong desires are likely to succeed. That's why sometimes we, believers, are defeated by these people, as even Jesus Christ was.

But we need to have strong faith and we need to persuade these people. So faith, love and invisible things are very important.

ALLEN

You said conditions, but I said selflessness. In my interpretation, my words must be "foundation" and not "condition."

Foundation. Foundation of success. It's not the condition.

Condition sometimes means materialistic and earthly condition; "if you get a lot of money," "if you succeed in your promotion," "if you become famous in the world" or things like that are the conditions. But my success doesn't mean something like that. I require love, of course, but it's a foundation, you know?

Its fundamental meaning...or, how should I say, it's earth itself. Earth means, in this meaning, the place where you seed your good causes. So, the problem is the foundation and not the conditions, I think. The foundation of your soul is very important and how you make your soul transparent and beautiful is essential.

There is no condition for that. Just think like how Jesus Christ thinks. Just think like how God thinks. Just think like how ancient prophets thought. Maybe the meaning of success and the meaning of happiness are quite different.

You are including the "flourish-ness" in this world. My success was very small and poor, so you don't regard my deeds as success or happiness. I died when I was 48 years old and I had little money. And when I was 15 years old, my father passed away. Am I successful or not, am I happy or not, if you think from the standpoint of conditions, I'm not happy and I'm not successful. But I think I'm happy and I'm successful.

5

Where Does Your Explanation of The Soul Come From?

ALLEN

Can you understand what I want to say, Filipino?

[*Audience laughs.*]

TOSHIHISA SAKAKIBARA

Thank you. By your words, I think I really understood what you wanted to say. That makes a real difference between Rhonda Byrne's *The Secret* and your thoughts.

I found that there are religious backgrounds in your life course or your words. Could you tell us about your life course and religious background that made you produce such a wonderful book?

ALLEN

Before that, I dare ask you: could you explain the difference between heart, mind and soul?

SAKAKIBARA

OK. That's a difficult question.

ALLEN

Not a difficult question. It's foundation.

SAKAKIBARA

OK. In Happy Science, we are learning about the heart, mind and soul.

ALLEN

Are they the same?

SAKAKIBARA

Not the same. Not really the same. The soul is our nature that God created. Our essence is the nature of God.

ALLEN

Nature of God? Hmm... Nature of God!? Please explain.

SAKAKIBARA

Our nature comes from God.

ALLEN

Oh, you are God? Ohh.

SAKAKIBARA

We are parts of God.

ALLEN

Parts of God!? Ohh. What kind of God?

SAKAKIBARA

We are children of God. Small, small ...cells.

ALLEN

Fragments, you mean?

SAKAKIBARA

Sorry? ...Ah, yes. Just a cell, small cells of God. But we are very confident of that.

ALLEN

Why?

SAKAKIBARA

Because we have the same nature that God has.

ALLEN

No. Why?

SAKAKIBARA

I don't know exactly, but...

ALLEN

Oh, you don't know!? Ohh.

SAKAKIBARA

God created us like that.

ALLEN

I can't believe that. Reality is the problem.

SAKAKIBARA

Reality? What do you mean by that?

ALLEN

Where does your reality come from? The source of your reality or confidence. Why can you say it? Is it just knowledge? Information? Is it written in books? Things like that?

SAKAKIBARA

Yes. Partially, it's true that we are only learning the knowledge in the first place. But we are disciplining ourselves to attain the true meaning of that. In the tremendous difficulties in your life course, it seems that you really grasped the true meaning of our nature or foundation.

ALLEN

I don't like the word "nature." Nature means "as it is."

SAKAKIBARA

OK. I will change that. Sorry. Foundation of life.

6

What is Eternal Life and Where is the Proof?

ALLEN

OK, OK. Filipino. I just want to say that you can attain the result through meditation only. While you are in meditation, you can see or feel the existence of God. Sometimes you are inspired by Him that exists in your soul.

But I can't say that you are a part of God, because if you want to say that, you must prove that. No one can understand about that.

ISHIKAWA

I think that the soul is eternal life given by God. And the heart...

ALLEN

You easily use the words "eternal life." What is eternal life?

ISHIKAWA

Eternal life is... We believe in the other world. So we reincarnate into this world...

ALLEN

Why is it eternal?

ISHIKAWA

"Why is it eternal?"

ALLEN

It is limited.

ISHIKAWA

Why is it limited?

ICHIKAWA

You are alive now in the spiritual world.

ISHIKAWA

You are the proof of eternal life.

ALLEN

No, no. Just 100 years. It's limited. Very limited.

ICHIKAWA

Humans reincarnate forever. You have many past lives and in the future, you will be reborn...

ALLEN

British people usually don't know and don't understand that argument.

ICHIKAWA

Unfortunately, it's because the disciples of Christianity omitted the teachings of reincarnation from the Bible. That's why so many Christian people do not know.

ALLEN

No one succeeded in proving your theory.

ICHIKAWA

I remember that Jesus Christ was told something like he is the second coming of Elijah in the Bible, so I'm sure this shows that he mentioned reincarnation.

ALLEN

Hmm, maybe so, but maybe not.

SAKAKIBARA

But it seems that you really understood the true meaning of eternal life, in your life. Could tell us about your experience?

ALLEN

God should have eternal life, I agree. But you humans have eternal life? If you want to say things like that, you must be a saint or God-like being. So, it's very difficult to use such kind of words.

Even I, James Allen, have only lived 100 years after death. Is it eternal life or not, I'm not sure. Today might be the last day of my life. If I say something wrong or something evil in my teachings, I will be perished by the Almighty God and that would be the end of my day. So, I cannot believe that I have eternal life. Because I am a human.

SAKAKIBARA

I see. Of course, I understand that it's all up to God because God created our souls and God decides whether we can live or not. These are all given. Yes, it's the truth.

But you really understood the meaning of life. So, could you tell us about your thoughts?

ALLEN

You cannot see my soul. You cannot understand my existence. You cannot hear my voice usually.

This is just a typical phenomenon of religious people

and historical saints. But if you were an English person, you would not believe that James Allen is saying something through the Japanese Master to the Japanese people. How can you prove that I'm James Allen?

SAKAKIBARA

For those people who have really read your books, I think they can feel it. They can *feel your* existence in this interview.

ALLEN

Failure!?

SAKAKIBARA

Ah, *feel*. Just...

ALLEN

Ah, *feel? Feel* and *failure* are the same...

SAKAKIBARA

[*Laughs.*] Just feeling your presence.

ALLEN

Ah, feeling is OK. It's OK.

7

Find Your Thinking Power and Use Your Willpower

ISHIKAWA

Can I ask another, different question?

ALLEN

OK.

ISHIKAWA

I think there are two types of philosophy to faith. One type is self-power or self-help.

ALLEN

Self-help type, OK.

ISHIKAWA

And the other is outside power type or philosophy relying on outside power. I think that Christianity maybe belongs to the outside power type. But you were born in England and many people there were Christians. Even so, you became a great master of self-help movement.

ALLEN

I'm not a great master [*laughs*].

ISHIKAWA

Why did you need self-help philosophy?

ALLEN

I just want to say that if you were poor, were born as a non-educated person or if your parents passed away early in your life, there is no condition for success and happiness.

But in your mind there is possibility for success. The key to success in your life is how to find your mind, I mean the thinking power which has direction. You must determine the final destination of your life and make effort to attain the result. And you can use your willpower at that time. This is the real key to success in your life.

This is a very simple teaching, but this very simple teaching cannot be understood by other people. People can easily understand how to get money, how to get position, how to make a great business or things like these. But I only worked on how to use the mind power. This is very difficult and it's usually mistaken for magical power like you said before. Who? "Attractive power" of...

ISHIKAWA

The law of attraction?

ALLEN

Law of attraction to Hell, you said?

ISHIKAWA

If you use it wrongly.

ALLEN

She recommended the law of attraction to Hell and it prevailed on earth, you said. But it's quite different.

I said earlier that we need purity, or to purify or *beautify* our mind. That is the point that is different from the attraction toward gravity of Hell.

8

Only One Percent of People Can Understand the Original Thinking Method of Self-Realization

ISHIKAWA

I see. So, according to your teachings, man is the maker of himself and the maker and shaper and author of his environment.

However, you said in another book, *Above Life's Turmoil*, that we cannot avoid the turmoil of the world. So, I would like to ask about the meaning of adversity, ordeal and turmoil. I think that maybe these are partially caused by our own thoughts, not all.

ALLEN

I'm a very small, small person. So, I cannot change other people's life courses. I have no such kind of power. I'm not Jesus Christ, so I have little power. I can just give some hints to the people who are suffering now.

But the real power to rebuild and remake your lives is in your mind only. Each and every person. I can just give some tips to them. I can only give them the hints. I cannot change their life courses and I cannot give any money, success or happiness myself. But they can get those if they want to be or if they imagine becoming such kind of person.

This is the original thinking method of self-realization. But it's very difficult. Only one percent of people can understand this theory. I'm afraid you [Ishikawa] fail my test.

ICHIKAWA

Thank you very much. As you said, only one percent of the population can acquire the power of thought. And we are just ordinary people.

ALLEN

Not ordinary. Small, small, small, small, very small being is the reality of humankind. God is great, but human is very, very small like an ant. This is the starting point. You said you are one of the gods or a part of God. No, no, no, no. You are going to Hell in the near future. Ha!

ICHIKAWA

OK. So, you mean, to realize the power of thought, we should first realize that we are small existences in front of God, right?

ALLEN

Yes. And small efforts. We are required small efforts, day by day.

9

Meditation:
The Only Way to Inner Happiness
And to the World of God

ALLEN

My success is not like the success of, for example, a millionaire on Wall Street with a very huge amount of assets. I'm not a millionaire, so my success is not the law to become a millionaire.

But I feel very, very happy in my mind because I'm filled with God's Light within me and I can give part of my light to other people. That is my success. That is my happiness.

So, if you define happiness as "to get something," success as "to get something from others, the government, the mass media, another country or something like that," and victory as something like "happiness," then that's a little different. I don't mean it like that. My happiness is "inner happiness."

ISHIKAWA

I think, to acquire such inner peace or inner happiness, maybe meditation is very important.

ALLEN

Yes, very important.

ISHIKAWA

And your wife said something like, "James Allen may truly be called the prophet of meditation." In your book, *The Way of Peace*, it says, "Spiritual meditation is the pathway to Divinity. It is the mystic ladder which reaches from earth to heaven, from error to Truth, from pain to peace. Every saint has climbed it." Why is meditation so important and how can we practice true meditation?

ALLEN

Yes, it's the only tool to go to the World of God. It's the bridge from this world to another world where God lives. To make the bridge, meaning the spiritual bridge, of course; to make the spiritual bridge, practice meditation.

Meditation requires daily efforts. You must make up your mind to continue your meditation every day. For example, in my case, I meditated early in the morning near a cliff by the sea, I mean the coast, or in the middle of a small mountain. Sometimes I had conversations with spiritual beings who might have been angels. Several experiences led me to pure faith in God.

God Himself cannot answer my question, but God's disciple in the heavenly world sometimes advised me and answered me regarding my poverty, illness, lack of money, spiritual problems, problems concerning my lack of education and regarding my confusion about hope. This is meditation.

10

The Way to Reconcile Wealth with Happiness

ICHIKAWA

Thank you. You didn't have much money when you were alive, but in the same age there were many people who were influenced by you, such as Dale Carnegie, Norman Vincent Peale, Napoleon Hill...

ALLEN

They are rich [*laughs*].

ICHIKAWA

Or Andrew Carnegie, Henry Ford or John Rockefeller. From your perspective, what do you think about these giant entrepreneurs?

ALLEN

They are rich and they became famous as the giants of humankind in the 20th century. But I am a small person. Just a small person. Not so famous and didn't have enough money. I only had enough money for my small family to live every day, only to ask for bread and butter and some wine or something like that. I was not rich. I was below ordinary people.

But through my *As a Man Thinketh*, there appeared a lot of successful people. They got money and grew rich. Some say, "Think and grow rich*." Yes, it's true.

But I'm sorry to say that they are not so successful in their mind. They are trapped by earthly desires, earthly success and earthly fame. I'm free from these desires and attractions. So, I'm peaceful in my mind and I'm happier than them.

ISHIKAWA

I think Jesus Christ declared, "No man can serve two masters" and "you cannot serve God and Mammon." So, how can we serve God?

ALLEN

Oh... you think much of yourself. You asked me how to serve God. It means you are next to God or near to God.

ISHIKAWA

I'm sorry.

---

* Title of Napoleon Hill's best-selling self-improvement book on success.

ALLEN

But... I cannot say at this point that you are next to God or a great disciple. Because you are a very earthly person. I felt like that.

ISHIKAWA

I need more meditation.

ALLEN

You have a lot of inner flame from the bottom of your heart. You want to acquire a lot of things through your life. You don't seek pureness and you don't want to *beautifly* your life. You are quite a different person and live in a different world. How is this a religious group? I cannot understand.

ISHIKAWA

I'm so sorry. But I would like you to answer my question for the sake of other people. In your book, you said that people have two masters, the self and the Truth, and they are always fighting against each other. So, how can we overcome such egotistical mind?

ALLEN

I think in this way. If you get money or success through gathering money, don't think that it's your money. It's the money of the people who are scheduled to be saved by God or the money for the poor people who are waiting for your aid. Don't think that the money is your own or that it belongs to your own religious group, or something like that. That is the only way to reconcile with God.

ISHIKAWA

Thank you so much.

11

Allen, One of the Tools of God, Became the Origin of New Thought

SAKAKIBARA

I would like to ask you about the reason why you were born in England...

ALLEN

Oh! Oh!

SAKAKIBARA

...in the middle of the 19th century. Why did you choose...

ALLEN

Why were you born in Japan?

SAKAKIBARA

Ah... for Happy Science.

ALLEN

Hmm, really?

SAKAKIBARA

Yes.

ALLEN

Really?

SAKAKIBARA

Yes, to serve Lord El Cantare, Master Ryuho Okawa.

ALLEN

But you did a lot of bad things in your life.

SAKAKIBARA

Yes. Yes, and I...

ALLEN

After that, you found Happy Science.

SAKAKIBARA

Yes.

ALLEN

So, you told a lie to me.

SAKAKIBARA

[*Laughs.*] I'm sorry. Umm... yes, I think that I really was bad before I met Happy Science. But that was part of my life plan. I regret that.

ALLEN

So, I will ask you again. "Why did James Allen have to be born in England?" Please ask your Lord about that.

SAKAKIBARA

Yes. OK. But you are in Heaven right now, in the Spirit World. You can recognize your true mission or the reason why you were born in England.

ALLEN

I don't know...

SAKAKIBARA

[*Laughs.*] Really?

ALLEN

...exactly. I was miserable in my life, [*laughs*] in the materialistic meaning.

SAKAKIBARA

But actually, I think your books became one of the main sources that developed the American prosperity. I think your books are related to the phenomenon [see Figure 1].

ALLEN

OK, I'll tell you the truth.

When I was in this world, I sometimes was guided by Jesus Christ and sometimes was guided by Buddha himself. This is the reason that James Allen was born in England. This is the reason that my philosophy influenced the United States

Figure 1.
Norman Vincent Peale (1898~1993) was an American minister and author. His book, *The Power of Positive Thinking* became a bestseller, selling 20 million copies worldwide.

of America and is spreading now through globalism and new Japanese religious movement.

Now, the Westerners and Oriental people are gathering together and are setting up one final goal of God. I was one of the tools of God like Mother Teresa or like that.

Of course, there were other prophets in the United States of America, for example, Napoleon Hill, Andrew Carnegie and Norman Vincent Peale. Norman Vincent Peale and I are very familiar in our relationship. We are aiming at attaining the same goal. Mr. Norman Vincent Peale did it in the United States of America and I was the origin of this New Thought* from England.

Yes, the starting point of this dream was very small, but now it's becoming a great river. Mr. Ryuho Okawa appeared in Japan and you have another mission; to reorganize this world which was divided by several religions and get them together again under the name of God. This is your mission, I guess.

SAKAKIBARA

Thank you very much for revealing such a spiritual secret for us.

---

* A religious movement affiliated mostly with Christianity that developed in 19th century United States. Teachings center around positive thinking such as "good thoughts bring good things."

12

The Paradox and Evil in Marx and Henry VIII

ICHIKAWA

In addition to that, do you have any spiritual secret to vanish Marxism in Europe? Because before you published your book, Karl Marx published *The Communist Manifesto* and in that age, Marxism and totalitarianism spread in Europe.

ALLEN

My power was so poor and my influence was so small. Karl Marx did a lot in this world because his thought was very similar to the wavelengths of this earthly world in the spiritual context. He just lived as a prophet of materialistic people.

People seek bread but don't seek the Truth of God these days. That's why he was greatly successful in this world. But now he is deprived of almost everything in another world*.

This is a paradox. The people who want to supply goods

---

* According to Happy Science spiritual readings, after Marx' death, he fell to a Hell for leaders who caused confusion for others by his philosophy. He has not yet realized that he is not alive. Refer to *Marx Motakuto no Spiritual Message* (literally, Spiritual Messages from Marx and Mao Zedong) [Tokyo: IRH Press, 2010].

and materialistic things in this world and want to make this world happier go to Hell and are deprived of a lot of property. And the people who live through meditation and get very small things in this world become greater in the spiritual realm. This is a paradox which also occurred in the age of Jesus Christ. I think so.

ICHIKAWA

Thank you very much. After you passed away, England...

ALLEN

Declined [*laughs*].

ICHIKAWA

...suffered from the British disease*. If you were in England now, what kind of message would you want to tell the people?

ALLEN

The Christianity of England is a little different from the real Christianity. The origin of the Church of England is not so

---

* The U.K. implemented its "from cradle to grave" social welfare policies after World War II, leading to an increase in social security cost and a drop in the people's motivation to work. As a result, the U.K. suffered serious economic downturn in the 1960s and 1970s. People around the world called this the British disease or the English disease.

good, I think. Henry VIII*, the founder of the British church, was a bad man. Not "batman," but "bad man."

His influence contaminated the Christianity of England and England's colonialism all over the world was contaminated by his evil thoughts. So, I must purify English Christianity. This was one of my missions. This is the answer to your question.

ICHIKAWA

In the modern society like the U.K., so many people emigrate from their own countries to the U.K. and get citizenship in the U.K. Do you have any advice for these immigrants to be successful or to attain happiness in foreign countries?

ALLEN

Ah... I can only see darkness in the future of the U.K. There needs new light in our future because the starting point of New Thought was 'lack of power.' I wrote 19 books, but my books... [*Looks at Ishikawa*] Oh, are you OK?

---

* Henry VIII (1491~1547) A king of England who was the second monarch from the House of Tudor. Following conflict over his divorce, he broke away from the Roman Catholic Church and established the Church of England. Henry VIII was married six times, and is believed to have been an egoistic and merciless king. The spirit of Princess Diana also mentions problems of Henry VIII in her spiritual message. Refer to *Spiritual Interview with Princess Diana* [Tokyo: HS Press, 2017].

[*Ishikawa passes out in his chair, facing toward the ceiling.*]

ALLEN

Huh? Are you OK? OK?

ICHIKAWA

Could you give us a rest?

ALLEN

Oh, sorry.

[*Staff helps Ishikawa recover and helps him leave his seat.*]

ALLEN

Oh, I'm a messenger from Hell. Sorry.

ICHIKAWA

I think your light was too strong.

ALLEN

Sorry. Uh-huh. His pride was hurt and...

ICHIKAWA

We're very sorry to interrupt your talking.

ALLEN

OK, I will go back soon, so, don't mind. This is the final session.

ICHIKAWA

It's quite precious time for us to talk to you so...

ALLEN

Is this precious? Really?

ICHIKAWA

Precious, yes.

ALLEN

Oh, I'm sorry. I questioned a lot about you, so you are confused.

ICHIKAWA

It's an honor to receive questions from you.

SAKAKIBARA

We appreciate it.

13

Why is it Difficult
To Practice Faith and Missionary Work?

ALLEN

Belief is very difficult. People easily use the words 'belief' and 'faith.' But in reality, people don't understand the real meaning of these words because they don't understand the reality of God or reality of sacred beings.

Some sacred beings come down to this earth to save a lot of people. People don't recognize these facts, so 'belief' and 'faith' for them are not correct, I think.

SAKAKIBARA

We will convey your true intentions to the people, along with the Happy Science teachings.

ALLEN

But you will find difficulties in the near future because you told a lot of people that El Cantare is the Father of Jesus Christ*. You must prove that. And how to prove that fact is

---

* Refer to *The Laws of Faith* [New York: IRH Press, 2018].

very difficult. If this was in the Medieval age, you would be burned to death because of your words. Even now, it's not so easy to convince people of such simple words.

Of course, think simply, but please think from the standpoints of a lot of people and have mercy toward the people who cannot believe in what you are saying. That's usually the case for common people who don't have real faith in their minds. So, it's very difficult to convey the Truth all over the U.K., Europe and the United States.

If you earned a lot of money or produced a money-making management method or something like that, it will be helpful for you. But if you teach only about the mind or how to purify your mind or *beautify* your life, that will bear no fruits, in reality, in the worldly meaning. So, you will feel a lot of difficulties in your missionary work.

14

Allen's Past Life

SAKAKIBARA

OK. I'm so thankful for you giving all of us precious advice. We will do our best to convey the Truth, including your teachings, to the people in England and people all over the world.

You had such a great mission in your life and this was already planned in Heaven. And you were inspired by Jesus Christ and Shakyamuni Buddha. If you don't mind, could you reveal your past incarnations?

ALLEN

Hmm... Saint Francis [see Figure 2 and 3] in Italy. At the time, I knew someone in this group. Maybe... Umm... someone who graduated from a Christian university.

ICHIKAWA

Mr. Oikawa*?

ALLEN

Mr. Oikawa, Oikawa, Oikawa, Oikawa, Ichikawa, Oikawa, Ichikawa... Ah, I don't know the difference. But someone who was my colleague at the time.

ICHIKAWA

Or Mr. Isono*? He's now in Europe.

ALLEN

Mr. Isono? He is like Buddha's belly†. Maybe a Buddhist or someone from Japanese Shintoism. Of course, a Christian person, too. But I don't exactly know about him. It might be you or something "kawa."

ICHIKAWA

Thank you.

---

* Oikawa and Isono are staff at Happy Science who once belonged to the International Headquarters.

† Hotei, one of the Seven Gods of Fortune, is said to have Buddha's belly in English.

SAKAKIBARA

Can we take it that you're guiding Happy Science University?

ALLEN

Guiding Happy Science University? You're asking me?

Figure 2.
Saint Francis (1181/82~1226) a Roman Catholic friar. Born in Assisi, Italy. Following Jesus Christ's footsteps, he lived a life of poverty and service and established the Franciscan Orders. Two years after his death, he was pronounced a saint by Pope Gregory IX. Pictured is the oldest image of Saint Francis still in existence (1223).

SAKAKIBARA

Yes.

ALLEN

Guide? Oh, it's difficult. I studied only through elementary school and middle school. That's all. I have no higher education, so I cannot. But in the spiritual meaning, I will aid you.

SAKAKIBARA

Please guide us and Happy Science University.

Figure 3.
The picture titled *Sermon to the Birds* (ca. 1290) by Giotto, depicting a famous episode where Saint Francis is giving a sermon to the birds.

ALLEN

OK, but don't forget. A greater person in this world does not mean he or she is greater in another world or God's world. A man who thinks he is not great and makes an effort, day by day, small efforts, day by day like an ant, becomes great in another world when he passes away.

So, please teach your students or followers to not think of themselves as great or big. Your starting point is very small and your work and efforts are very small. But you can accumulate these deeds, day by day. In the end, a tree will bear a lot of fruits in this world or in the other world. Only God knows the result.

But this is belief. This is faith. Don't examine your success or happiness through the result of this world only. OK?

15

Walk When the Light is Shining

SAKAKIBARA

Yes. Thank you very much. I think there is a strong spiritual connection between your soul and Happy Science.

ALLEN

I think so.

SAKAKIBARA

Could you also reveal your relationship with Lord El Cantare?

ALLEN

Of course, of course, of course. Of course.

ICHIKAWA

Could you disclose any part of the secret?

[SOMEONE IN AUDIENCE] Buddhist? Buddhist?

SAKAKIBARA

Were you also born as a Buddhist?

ALLEN

Yes, one of the disciples of Buddha.

SAKAKIBARA

Could you reveal the name?

ICHIKAWA

Among the ten disciples?

ALLEN

No, no, no. I'm a very small ant, so no one [in my past lives] is of a very famous name. I'm not a king level or queen level ant. Don't ask me about that. I'm a small disciple of Buddha. And a small disciple of Jesus Christ.

ICHIKAWA

During this conversation, I felt like I was talking to Lev Tolstoy*, if I'm not wrong.

---

* Happy Science has recorded Tolstoy's spiritual message. Ichikawa was one of the interviewers. Refer to *Tolstoy - Jinsei ni Okuru Kotoba* (literally, Tolstoy - Words for Life)[Tokyo: IRH Press, 2012].

ALLEN

Ah, Lev Tolstoy.

ICHIKAWA

He also said human beings are very small. You are interested in Lev Tolstoy. In the Bible it says something like, "Believe in the light while you have it, so that you will be the people of light." Do you have any relationship with Tolstoy?

ALLEN

Yes, I agree.

Please walk when the light is shining,

When the sun is shining.

It means that, when your Lord is in this world,

You must walk and walk

And complete your work.

Now is the day of daylight of God.

Please teach and let them know

About the rebirth of the Savior

In the country of Japan.

He wants to save the people of the world.

Now is the daytime.

Now is under the daylight of God.

So, now is your time to work.

SAKAKIBARA

Thank you very much.

16

Keep Purity of Mind and Selflessness As You Prosper and Progress

ICHIKAWA

Thank you. Sorry, the next one is our last question. In terms of belief, what is El Cantare to you?

ALLEN

El Cantare is the sunshine. He is the sunshine. The spiritual meaning of sunshine itself. So, He is not the Father of Jesus Christ. Father is a human. El Cantare is not a human. He is the spiritual sunshine of another world. It's the spring of spiritual power.

No one can define Him. You will be made to know about the secret of His miracle in the near future. He can do more and more great deeds in the near future, in 10 or 20 years.

At that time, don't be behind Him. Don't forget to awaken to the real meaning of His Truth. He is the Light of Heaven. Yes. Light itself.

ICHIKAWA & SAKAKIBARA

Thank you very much.

ICHIKAWA

Thank you very much. Our time is up, so we have to finish our conversation. We really appreciate you coming here. And I hope you will kindly guide Happy Science University and Happy Science Group. We will prosper and also make the world happy.

ALLEN

On the concept of prosperity, you want to teach people the concept of prosperity and progress. At that time, be careful. At the same time, please teach them the purity of mind and the importance of selflessness. It's very important.

To become great people is helpful in succeeding in this world, but this success sometimes makes them selfish or egoistic, so be careful about that.

Please purify your mind or *beautifly* your life through meditation. And sometimes be empty about everything in your life. That's very important.

And please give some kind words to that person who "fell down to earth" [the interviewer who left the seat]. He experienced a shock like Paul's. I pointed out his tendency, so he was shocked. But it will be helpful to him. Be kind to him. He is not a bad man. Please be kind to him.

SAKAKIBARA

Thank you very much for your kind words.

ALLEN

Thank you very much.

ICHIKAWA

Thank you very much.

17

After the Spiritual Interview

RYUHO OKAWA

[*Claps once.*] Thank you, James Allen. Thank you very much.

He is, of course, a religious person and he understood Buddhism and Christianity. It felt like he, himself, is a philosopher. In some meaning, he's a philosopher. He questioned your faith and the recognition about your religion. This was a hard test.

We recently had this kind of experience through Hannah Arendt*. They are severe now. They want to ask us whether we are qualified to join in this kind of session. So, we must be diligent in our daily work and studies. I think so.

Thank you very much today.

---

* Happy Science has recorded the spiritual message of political philosopher, Hannah Arendt. The interviewers received a tough oral examination from her. Refer to *On Happiness Revolution: A Spiritual Interview with Hannah Arendt* [Tokyo: HS Press, 2014].

ABOUT THE AUTHOR

Founder and CEO of Happy Science Group.

Ryuho Okawa was born on July 7th 1956, in Tokushima, Japan. After graduating from the University of Tokyo with a law degree, he joined a Tokyo-based trading house. While working at its New York headquarters, he studied international finance at the Graduate Center of the City University of New York. In 1981, he attained Great Enlightenment and became aware that he is El Cantare with a mission to bring salvation to all humankind.

In 1986, he established Happy Science. It now has members in over 165 countries across the world, with more than 700 branches and temples as well as 10,000 missionary houses around the world.

He has given over 3,400 lectures (of which more than 150 are in English) and published over 3,000 books (of which more than 600 are Spiritual Interview Series), and many are translated into 40 languages. Along with *The Laws of the Sun* and *The Laws Of Messiah*, many of the books have become best sellers or million sellers. To date, Happy Science has produced 25 movies. The original story and original concept were given by the Executive Producer Ryuho Okawa. He has also composed music and written lyrics of over 450 pieces.

Moreover, he is the Founder of Happy Science University and Happy Science Academy (Junior and Senior High School), Founder and President of the Happiness Realization Party, Founder and Honorary Headmaster of Happy Science Institute of Government and Management, Founder of IRH Press Co., Ltd., and the Chairperson of NEW STAR PRODUCTION Co., Ltd. and ARI Production Co., Ltd.

WHAT IS EL CANTARE?

El Cantare means "the Light of the Earth," and is the Supreme God of the Earth who has been guiding humankind since the beginning of Genesis. He is whom Jesus called Father and Muhammad called Allah, and is *Ame-no-Mioya-Gami*, Japanese Father God. Different parts of El Cantare's core consciousness have descended to Earth in the past, once as Alpha and another as Elohim. His branch spirits, such as Shakyamuni Buddha and Hermes, have descended to Earth many times and helped to flourish many civilizations. To unite various religions and to integrate various fields of study in order to build a new civilization on Earth, a part of the core consciousness has descended to Earth as Master Ryuho Okawa.

Alpha is a part of the core consciousness of El Cantare who descended to Earth around 330 million years ago. Alpha preached Earth's Truths to harmonize and unify Earth-born humans and space people who came from other planets.

Elohim is a part of El Cantare's core consciousness who descended to Earth around 150 million years ago. He gave wisdom, mainly on the differences of light and darkness, good and evil.

Ame-no-Mioya-Gami (Japanese Father God) is the Creator God and the Father God who appears in the ancient literature, *Hotsuma Tsutae*. It is believed that He descended on the foothills of Mt. Fuji about 30,000 years ago and built the Fuji dynasty, which is the root of the Japanese civilization. With justice as the central pillar, Ame-no-Mioya-Gami's teachings spread to ancient civilizations of other countries in the world.

Shakyamuni Buddha was born as a prince into the Shakya Clan in India around 2,600 years ago. When he was 29 years old, he renounced the world and sought enlightenment. He later attained Great Enlightenment and founded Buddhism.

Hermes is one of the 12 Olympian gods in Greek mythology, but the spiritual Truth is that he taught the teachings of love and progress around 4,300 years ago that became the origin of the current Western civilization. He is a hero that truly existed.

Ophealis was born in Greece around 6,500 years ago and was the leader who took an expedition to as far as Egypt. He is the God of miracles, prosperity, and arts, and is known as Osiris in the Egyptian mythology.

Rient Arl Croud was born as a king of the ancient Incan Empire around 7,000 years ago and taught about the mysteries of the mind. In the heavenly world, he is responsible for the interactions that take place between various planets.

Thoth was an almighty leader who built the golden age of the Atlantic civilization around 12,000 years ago. In the Egyptian mythology, he is known as god Thoth.

Ra Mu was a leader who built the golden age of the civilization of Mu around 17,000 years ago. As a religious leader and a politician, he ruled by uniting religion and politics.

WHAT IS A SPIRITUAL MESSAGE?

We are all spiritual beings living on this earth. The following is the mechanism behind Master Ryuho Okawa's spiritual messages.

1 You are a spirit

People are born into this world to gain wisdom through various experiences and return to the other world when their lives end. We are all spirits and repeat this cycle in order to refine our souls.

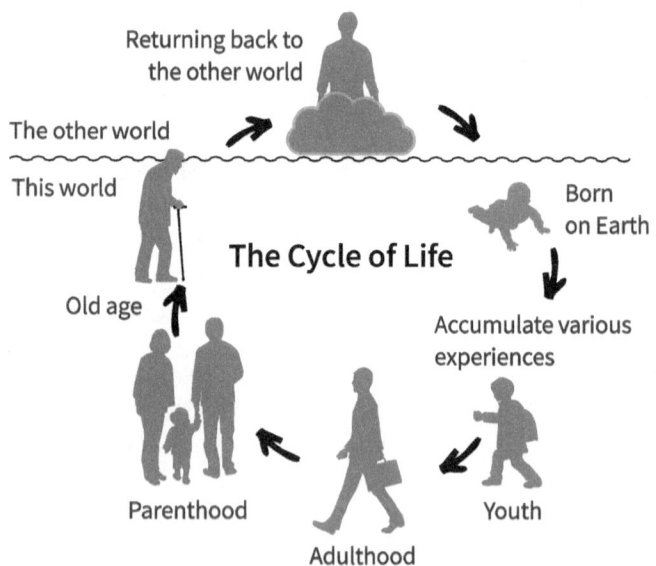

Returning back to
the other world

The other world

This world

Born
on Earth

The Cycle of Life

Old age

Accumulate various
experiences

Parenthood

Adulthood

Youth

2 You have a guardian spirit

Guardian spirits are those who protect the people who are living on this earth. Each of us has a guardian spirit that watches over us and guides us from the other world. They were us in our past life, and are identical in how we think.

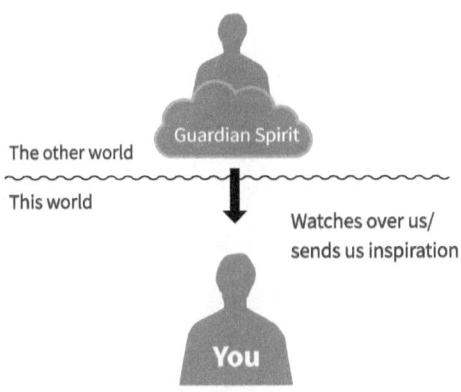

3 How spiritual messages work

Master Ryuho Okawa, through his enlightenment, is capable of summoning any spirit from anywhere in the world, including the spirit world.

Master Okawa's way of receiving spiritual messages is fundamentally different from that of other psychic mediums who undergo trances and are thereby completely taken over by the spirits they are channeling.

Master Okawa's attainment of a high level of enlightenment enables him to retain full control of his consciousness and body throughout the duration of the spiritual message. To allow the spirits to express their own thoughts and personalities freely, however, Master Okawa usually softens the dominancy of his consciousness. This way, he is able to keep his own philosophies out of the way and ensure that the spiritual messages are pure expressions of the spirits he is channeling.

Since guardian spirits think at the same subconscious level as the person living on earth, Master Okawa can summon the spirit and find out what the person on earth is actually thinking. If the person has already returned to the other world, the spirit can give messages to the people living on earth through Master Okawa.

Since 2009, many spiritual messages have been openly recorded by Master Okawa and published. Spiritual messages from the guardian spirits of people living today such as Donald Trump, former Japanese Prime Minister Shinzo Abe and Chinese President Xi Jinping, as well as spiritual messages sent from the spirit world by Jesus Christ, Muhammad, Thomas Edison, Mother Teresa, Steve Jobs and Nelson Mandela are just a tiny pack of spiritual messages that were published so far.

Domestically, in Japan, these spiritual messages are being read by a wide range of politicians and mass media, and the high-level contents of these books are delivering an impact even more on politics, news and public opinion. In recent years, there have been spiritual messages recorded in English, and

English translations are being done on the spiritual messages given in Japanese. These have been published overseas, one after another, and have started to shake the world.

1 The guardian spirit / spirit in the other world...

2 Goes inside Master Okawa in this world

3 Master Okawa speaks the words of the guardian spirit / spirit

For more about spiritual messages and a complete list of books in the Spiritual Interview Series, visit okawabooks.com

ABOUT HAPPY SCIENCE

Happy Science is a global movement that empowers individuals to find purpose and spiritual happiness and to share that happiness with their families, societies, and the world. With more than 12 million members around the world, Happy Science aims to increase awareness of spiritual truths and expand our capacity for love, compassion, and joy so that together we can create the kind of world we all wish to live in.

Activities at Happy Science are based on the Principle of Happiness (Love, Wisdom, Self-Reflection, and Progress). This principle embraces worldwide philosophies and beliefs, transcending boundaries of culture and religions.

Love teaches us to give ourselves freely without expecting anything in return; it encompasses giving, nurturing, and forgiving.

Wisdom leads us to the insights of spiritual truths, and opens us to the true meaning of life and the will of God (the universe, the highest power, Buddha).

Self-Reflection brings a mindful, nonjudgmental lens to our thoughts and actions to help us find our truest selves—the essence of our souls—and deepen our connection to the highest power. It helps us attain a clean and peaceful mind and leads us to the right life path.

Progress emphasizes the positive, dynamic aspects of our spiritual growth—actions we can take to manifest and spread happiness around the world. It's a path that not only expands our soul growth, but also furthers the collective potential of the world we live in.

PROGRAMS AND EVENTS

The doors of Happy Science are open to all. We offer a variety of programs and events, including self-exploration and self-growth programs, spiritual seminars, meditation and contemplation sessions, study groups, and book events.

Our programs are designed to:
* Deepen your understanding of your purpose and meaning in life
* Improve your relationships and increase your capacity to love unconditionally
* Attain peace of mind, decrease anxiety and stress, and feel positive
* Gain deeper insights and a broader perspective on the world
* Learn how to overcome life's challenges
  ... and much more.

For more information, visit <u>happy-science.org</u>.

CONTACT INFORMATION

Happy Science is a worldwide organization with branches and temples around the globe. For a comprehensive list, visit the worldwide directory at *happy-science.org*. The following are some of the many Happy Science locations:

UNITED STATES AND CANADA

New York
79 Franklin St., New York, NY 10013, USA
Phone: 1-212-343-7972
Fax: 1-212-343-7973
Email: ny@happy-science.org
Website: happyscience-usa.org

New Jersey
66 Hudson St., #2R, Hoboken, NJ 07030, USA
Phone: 1-201-313-0127
Email: nj@happy-science.org
Website: happyscience-usa.org

Chicago
2300 Barrington Rd., Suite #400,
Hoffman Estates, IL 60169, USA
Phone: 1-630-937-3077
Email: chicago@happy-science.org
Website: happyscience-usa.org

Florida
5208 8th St., Zephyrhills, FL 33542, USA
Phone: 1-813-715-0000
Fax: 1-813-715-0010
Email: florida@happy-science.org
Website: happyscience-usa.org

Atlanta
1874 Piedmont Ave., NE Suite 360-C
Atlanta, GA 30324, USA
Phone: 1-404-892-7770
Email: atlanta@happy-science.org
Website: happyscience-usa.org

San Francisco
525 Clinton St.
Redwood City, CA 94062, USA
Phone & Fax: 1-650-363-2777
Email: sf@happy-science.org
Website: happyscience-usa.org

Los Angeles
1590 E. Del Mar Blvd., Pasadena, CA
91106, USA
Phone: 1-626-395-7775
Fax: 1-626-395-7776
Email: la@happy-science.org
Website: happyscience-usa.org

Orange County
16541 Gothard St. Suite 104
Huntington Beach, CA 92647
Phone: 1-714-659-1501
Email: oc@happy-science.org
Website: happyscience-usa.org

San Diego
7841 Balboa Ave. Suite #202
San Diego, CA 92111, USA
Phone: 1-626-395-7775
Fax: 1-626-395-7776
E-mail: sandiego@happy-science.org
Website: happyscience-usa.org

Hawaii
Phone: 1-808-591-9772
Fax: 1-808-591-9776
Email: hi@happy-science.org
Website: happyscience-usa.org

Kauai
3343 Kanakolu Street, Suite 5
Lihue, HI 96766, USA
Phone: 1-808-822-7007
Fax: 1-808-822-6007
Email: kauai-hi@happy-science.org
Website: happyscience-usa.org

Toronto

845 The Queensway
Etobicoke, ON M8Z 1N6, Canada
Phone: 1-416-901-3747
Email: toronto@happy-science.org
Website: happy-science.ca

Vancouver

#201-2607 East 49th Avenue,
Vancouver, BC, V5S 1J9, Canada
Phone: 1-604-437-7735
Fax: 1-604-437-7764
Email: vancouver@happy-science.org
Website: happy-science.ca

INTERNATIONAL

Tokyo

1-6-7 Togoshi, Shinagawa,
Tokyo, 142-0041, Japan
Phone: 81-3-6384-5770
Fax: 81-3-6384-5776
Email: tokyo@happy-science.org
Website: happy-science.org

Seoul

74, Sadang-ro 27-gil,
Dongjak-gu, Seoul, Korea
Phone: 82-2-3478-8777
Fax: 82-2-3478-9777
Email: korea@happy-science.org
Website: happyscience-korea.org

London

3 Margaret St.
London, W1W 8RE United Kingdom
Phone: 44-20-7323-9255
Fax: 44-20-7323-9344
Email: eu@happy-science.org
Website: www.happyscience-uk.org

Taipei

No. 89, Lane 155, Dunhua N. Road,
Songshan District, Taipei City 105, Taiwan
Phone: 886-2-2719-9377
Fax: 886-2-2719-5570
Email: taiwan@happy-science.org
Website: happyscience-tw.org

Sydney

516 Pacific Highway, Lane Cove North,
2066 NSW, Australia
Phone: 61-2-9411-2877
Fax: 61-2-9411-2822
Email: sydney@happy-science.org

Kuala Lumpur

No 22A, Block 2, Jalil Link Jalan Jalil
Jaya 2, Bukit Jalil 57000,
Kuala Lumpur, Malaysia
Phone: 60-3-8998-7877
Fax: 60-3-8998-7977
Email: malaysia@happy-science.org
Website: happyscience.org.my

Sao Paulo

Rua. Domingos de Morais 1154,
Vila Mariana, Sao Paulo SP
CEP 04010-100, Brazil
Phone: 55-11-5088-3800
Email: sp@happy-science.org
Website: happyscience.com.br

Kathmandu

Kathmandu Metropolitan City,
Ward No. 15, Ring Road, Kimdol,
Sitapaila Kathmandu, Nepal
Phone: 977-1-427-2931
Email: nepal@happy-science.org

Jundiai

Rua Congo, 447, Jd. Bonfiglioli
Jundiai-CEP, 13207-340, Brazil
Phone: 55-11-4587-5952
Email: jundiai@happy-science.org

Kampala

Plot 877 Rubaga Road, Kampala
P.O. Box 34130 Kampala, UGANDA
Phone: 256-79-4682-121
Email: uganda@happy-science.org

ABOUT HAPPINESS REALIZATION PARTY

The Happiness Realization Party (HRP) was founded in May 2009 by Master Ryuho Okawa as part of the Happy Science Group. HRP strives to improve the Japanese society, based on three basic political principles of "freedom, democracy, and faith," and let Japan promote individual and public happiness from Asia to the world as a leader nation.

1) Diplomacy and Security: Protecting Freedom, Democracy, and Faith of Japan and the World from China's Totalitarianism

Japan's current defense system is insufficient against China's expanding hegemony and the threat of North Korea's nuclear missiles. Japan, as the leader of Asia, must strengthen its defense power and promote strategic diplomacy together with the nations which share the values of freedom, democracy, and faith. Further, HRP aims to realize world peace under the leadership of Japan, the nation with the spirit of religious tolerance.

2) Economy: Early economic recovery through utilizing the "wisdom of the private sector"

Economy has been damaged severely by the novel coronavirus originated in China. Many companies have been forced into bankruptcy or out of business. What is needed for economic recovery now is not subsidies and regulations by the government, but policies which can utilize the "wisdom of the private sector."

For more information, visit en.hr-party.jp

HAPPY SCIENCE ACADEMY JUNIOR AND SENIOR HIGH SCHOOL

Happy Science Academy Junior and Senior High School is a boarding school founded with the goal of educating the future leaders of the world who can have a big vision, persevere, and take on new challenges.

Currently, there are two campuses in Japan; the Nasu Main Campus in Tochigi Prefecture, founded in 2010, and the Kansai Campus in Shiga Prefecture, founded in 2013.

Nasu Main Campus

Kansai Campus

ABOUT HS PRESS

HS Press is an imprint of IRH Press Co., Ltd. IRH Press Co., Ltd., based in Tokyo, was founded in 1987 as a publishing division of Happy Science. IRH Press publishes religious and spiritual books, journals, magazines and also operates broadcast and film production enterprises. For more information, visit *okawabooks.com*.

Follow us on:

f Facebook: Okawa Books   ⊙ Instagram: OkawaBooks
▶ Youtube: Okawa Books   🐦 Twitter: Okawa Books
𝓟 Pinterest: Okawa Books   g Goodreads: Ryuho Okawa

——— **NEWSLETTER** ———

To receive book related news, promotions and events, please subscribe to our newsletter below.

∞ eepurl.com/bsMeJj

——— **AUDIO / VISUAL MEDIA** ———

YOUTUBE

PODCAST

Introduction of Ryuho Okawa's titles; topics ranging from self-help, current affairs, spirituality, religion, and the universe.

BOOKS BY RYUHO OKAWA

THE LAWS OF MISSION

Essential Truths For Spiritual Awakening in a Secular Age

In this day and age of advanced scientific and information technology, we are often deluded by a false sense that we know everything. But in fact, many people cannot even answer simple but fundamental questions about life, such as "what's the purpose of our life" and "what happens after death."

In this book, Ryuho Okawa offers integral spiritual truths that bring about spiritual awakening within each of us. This book helps us find the purpose and meaning of our life and make the right decisions so that we can walk on the path to happiness.

For a complete list of books, visit okawabooks.com

THE LAWS OF JUSTICE

HOW WE CAN SOLVE
WORLD CONFLICTS & BRING PEACE

How can we solve conflicts in this world? Why is it that we continue to live in a world of turmoil, when we all wish to live in a world of peace and harmony?

In recent years, we've faced issues that jeopardize international peace and security, including the rise of ISIS, Syrian civil war and refugee crisis, break-off of diplomatic relations between Saudi Arabia and Iran, Russia's annexation of Crimea, China's military expansion, and North Korea's nuclear development.

This book shows what global justice is from a comprehensive perspective of the Supreme God. Becoming aware of this view will let us embrace differences in beliefs, recognize other people's divine nature, and love and forgive one another. It will also become the key to solving the issues we face, whether they're religious, political, societal, economic, or academic, and help the world become a better and safer world for all of us living today.

For a complete list of books, visit okawabooks.com

THE TRUMP SECRET

SEEING THROUGH THE PAST, PRESENT, AND FUTURE OF THE NEW AMERICAN PRESIDENT

Donald Trump's victory in the 2016 presidential election surprised almost all major vote forecasters who predicted Hillary Clinton's victory. But 10 months earlier, in January 2016, Ryuho Okawa, Global Visionary, a renowned spiritual leader, and international best-selling author, had already foreseen Trump's victory. This book contains a series of lectures and interviews that unveil the secrets to Trump's victory and makes predictions of what will happen under his presidency. This book predicts the coming of a new America that will go through a great transformation from the "red and blue states" to the United States.

CONTENTS

For a complete list of books, visit okawabooks.com

INTO THE STORM OF INTERNATIONAL POLITICS

THE NEW STANDARDS OF THE WORLD ORDER

The world is now seeking a new idea or a new philosophy that will show the countries with such values the direction they should head in. In this book, Okawa presents new standards of the world order while giving his own analysis on world affairs concerning the U.S., China, Islamic State and others.

1 My Current Opinion on International Politics

2 Indicating Global Trends and the Prospects of a "New World Order"

3 Contentious Issues with South Korea and the Diplomatic Stance Japan Should Adopt

4 The Direction that the Anti-China Demo in Hong Kong is Heading in And its Effect on the International Community

5 The Future of Islamic State and the Mission of Happy Science

---

For a complete list of books, visit okawabooks.com

THE DECISION TOWARD PROSPERITY

THE TRUMP REVOLUTION
WILL CHANGE THE WORLD

"Trump Revolution" is a term also used by other authors, not just Ryuho Okawa, but he is one of the authors who see through the essence of this revolution the most. How so? Okawa foresaw the birth of President Trump, as early as in January 2016.

Okawa, a Global Visionary, clearly sees where the world is headed and how the people in each country should think and act for the world to enjoy a better future. As the opinions by experts on American politics or international politics are in disarray, you could say that this book has pointed out the principal pillar of thought.

In the book, Okawa talks a lot about Japanese politics as Japan is his mother country, but the universal philosophy behind his words will surely enlighten readers in other countries, too. This is the guidebook that will help the world realize prosperity for the next 300 years.

For a complete list of books, visit okawabooks.com

THE LAWS OF THE SUN

ONE SOURCE, ONE PLANET, ONE PEOPLE

IMAGINE IF YOU COULD ASK GOD why He created this world and what spiritual laws He used to shape us—and everything around us. If we could understand His designs and intentions, we could discover what our goals in life should be and whether our actions move us closer to those goals or farther away.

THE GOLDEN LAWS

HISTORY THROUGH
THE EYES OF THE ETERNAL BUDDHA

The Golden Laws reveals how Buddha's Plan has been unfolding on earth, and outlines five thousand years of the secret history of humankind. Once we understand the true course of history, we cannot help but become aware of the significance of our spiritual mission in the present age.

THE NINE DIMENSIONS

UNVEILING THE LAWS OF ETERNITY

This book is a window into the mind of our loving God, who encourages us to grow into greater angels. It reveals His deepest intentions, answering the timely question of why He conceived such a colorful medley of religions, philosophies, sciences, arts, and other forms of expression.

For a complete list of books, visit okawabooks.com

SPIRITUAL INTERVIEW WITH BRUCE LEE

THE RESURRECTION OF THE DRAGON

Here, we present you, martial artists and Bruce Lee fans all over the world who respect him even after his death over 40 years ago, the truth revealed by the "Dragon" who is still fighting evil in the Spirit World. He speaks a lot about his own kung fu philosophy that he had deepened further after his death, as well as the truth of his young death and the mission of his soul.

WHAT'S YOUR AIM, KIM JONG-UN?

REVEALING HIS MOST RECENT THOUGHTS

"It would be like a dream if the mass media in the world, including Japan, were permitted to conduct a completely exclusive interview with Kim Jong-un now. Although a spiritual coverage,
this book realized over 70% of that wish."

-From the Preface

SPIRITUAL INTERVIEW WITH THE GUARDIAN SPIRIT OF MALALA YOUSAFZAI

A WIND OF HOPE FOR THE ISLAMIC WORLD

This is the spiritual interview with the youngest Nobel Peace Prize laureate, Malala Yousafzai's guardian spirit. Learn about where her unyeilding courage and strength springs from and the vision and her vision that she has for the future.

For a complete list of books, visit okawabooks.com

Donald Trump vs. Kim Jong-un
A Spiritual Battle between Two Leaders

Who will pull the trigger first, Kim Jong-un or Donald Trump? The North Korean issue is entering the final phase. This book tells Kim Jong-un's scenario and the crucial points of Donald Trump's strategy. Here is the top-secret information to the North Korean issue.

Spiritual Interview with Liu Xiaobo
The Fight for Freedom Continues

On July 21, 2017, 8 days after his death, the spirit of Liu Xiaobo was resurrected to deliver his messages. This book reveals the truths about China, a totalitarian country that doesn't grant freedom to its people. In this book, the Chinese Nobel Prize winner shares his wish to hand down the movement of China's democratization to future generations.

Spiritual Interview with Princess Diana
Her messages, 20 years after her death

This spiritual message tells us about the background of the Paris accident and what Diana has been doing since her death. Diana said that through the spiritual conversation, she was able to deepen her understanding on the Spirit World and her own soul, and that she gained the key to return to the world of goddesses in Heaven.

For a complete list of books, visit okawabooks.com

THE NEW DIPLOMATIC STRATEGIES OF SIR WINSTON CHURCHILL

A SPIRITUAL INTERVIEW WITH THE FORMER PRIME MINISTER REGARDING THE AGE OF PERSEVERANCE

If there is a chance to hear the opinion of Sir Winston Churchill on current international affairs, journalists around the world will probably be interested to hear this. This book made this possible.

MARGARET THATCHER'S MIRACULOUS MESSAGE

AN INTERVIEW WITH THE IRON LADY 19 HOURS AFTER HER DEATH

On April 9, 2013, just nineteen hours after Margaret Thatcher's death, Master Okawa summoned her spirit to hold a spiritual interview. Her words will prove helpful not only to the United Kingdom, but also to the global economy and governments all over the world, including those of the United States and the European Union.

ON HAPPINESS REVOLUTION

A SPIRITUAL INTERVIEW WITH HANNAH ARENDT

In this book, the German-born Jewish American political theorist offers a spiritual lecture on democracy, on totalitarianism in East Asia, on communism and equality, on the Love of God and Justice of God, as well as her mission as a prophet of the new age.

For a complete list of books, visit okawabooks.com

CRITIQUE OF CURRENT WORLD AFFAIRS
IMMANUEL KANT'S ADVICE FROM HEAVEN

"We can clearly see from Kant's message that we constantly need to enlighten people in order to prevent humankind from falling into a dangerous, hellish way of thinking."

-From Preface

[This book is available only in local branches and temples of Happy Science. Please refer to the contact information.]

NELSON MANDELA'S LAST MESSAGE TO THE WORLD
A CONVERSATION WITH MADIBA SIX HOURS AFTER HIS DEATH

As Mandela's spirit says in this spiritual interview, God created our souls as thinking energy without color, and that our colorless soul is the basis of our fundamental freedom and equality. In this spiritual interview, Master Ryuho Okawa gives us a glimpse into the mind of this great leader whose undefeated spirit is a message of hope to us all.

INTERVIEWING THE GUARDIAN SPIRIT OF U.S AMBASSADOR CAROLINE KENNEDY

A NEW BRIDGE BETWEEN JAPAN AND THE U.S.

What is Ambassador Kennedy's views on Japan-U.S. and Japan-China relations? How does she view World War II? What was the reason behind the Kennedy tragedies? What does she seek from the Japanese and American people? Find the answers in this book.

For a complete list of books, visit okawabooks.com

Ryuho Okawa
- A Political Revolutionary

The Originator of Abenomics and Father of the Happiness Realization Party

In this book, the Founder and the Master of Happy Science Group as well as the Father of Happiness Realization Party, Master Okawa lays down the guiding principles and the ways to breakthrough on the topics of economy, finance, nuclear power plant, foreign diplomacy, social welfare, and society with aging population and a falling birth rate.

The Manifesto of the Happiness Realization Party

This book is a historical declaration to change the world through a peaceful revolution by the philosophy and speech based on the Truth, rather than by violence or massacre. It also states on the assessment of the meaning of WWII as well as how the relation between religion and politics should be. It is a must read for all people who wish to build a true utopia.

The Power to Lead the World

"It is not enough to speak only of ideals; we must envision how this world should be while setting our eyes firmly on things like real politics."

-Master Ryuho Okawa

[This book is available only in local branches and temples of Happy Science. Please refer to the contact information.]

For a complete list of books, visit okawabooks.com

THE STARTING POINT OF HAPPINESS

AN INSPIRING GUIDE TO POSITIVE LIVING WITH FAITH, LOVE, AND COURAGE

In *The Starting Point of Happiness*, author Ryuho Okawa awakens us to the true spiritual values of our life; he beautifully illustrates, in simple but profound words, how we can find purpose and meaning in life and attain happiness that lasts forever.

THE LAWS OF SUCCESS

A SPIRITUAL GUIDE TO TURNING YOUR HOPES INTO REALITY

This is a basic introduction to the teachings of Ryuho Okawa, illustrating his core philosophy. He shows you how to free yourself from the suffering of selfish love; how to stop bemoaning your ignorance and learn through study how to cut off negative spiritual influences through self-reflection; and how your strong thoughts will be realized.

THE LAWS OF HAPPINESS

THE FOUR PRINCIPLES FOR A SUCCESSFUL LIFE

This is a basic introduction to the teachings of Ryuho Okawa, illustrating his core philosophy. He shows you how to free yourself from the suffering of selfish love; how to stop bemoaning your ignorance and learn through study how to cut off negative spiritual influences through self-reflection; and how your strong thoughts will be realized.

For a complete list of books, visit okawabooks.com

TIPS TO FIND HAPPINESS

CREATING A HARMONIOUS HOME FOR YOUR SPOUSE, YOUR CHILDREN, AND YOURSELF

This is a series of questions and answers on common problems in marriage, work, and relationships, offering a wide range of both practical and spiritual suggestions that will be sure to resonate with everyone who has experienced difficulties in the home.

GUIDEPOSTS TO HAPPINESS

PRESCRIPTIONS FOR A WONDERFUL LIFE

In this book, author and spiritual leader Ryuho Okawa describes in detail some of the negative patterns of thinking that keep us from attaining peace of mind. He outlines the causes of a number of life's problems, including depression, inferiority complexes and conflicts that result from over-assertiveness. In this book, you will find many hints to help you solve your worries and attain true happiness.

INVINCIBLE THINKING

AN ESSENTIAL GUIDE FOR A LIFETIME OF GROWTH, SUCCESS, AND TRIUMPH

In this book, Ryuho Okawa lays out the principles of invincible thinking that will allow us to achieve long-lasting triumph. This powerful and unique philosophy is not only about becoming successful or achieving our goal in life, but also about building the foundation of life that becomes the basis of our life-long, lasting success and happiness.

For a complete list of books, visit okawabooks.com

THE LAWS OF WISDOM
SHINE YOUR DIAMOND WITHIN

This book guides you along the path on how to acquire wisdom, so that you can break through any wall you are facing or will confront in your life or in your business. By reading this book, you will be able to avoid getting lost in the flood of information and go beyond the level of just amassing knowledge. You will be able to come up with many great ideas, make effective planning and strategy and develop your leadership skills.

THE LAWS OF PERSEVERANCE
REVERSING YOUR COMMON SENSE

"No matter how much you suffer, the Truth will gradually shine forth as you continue to endure hardships. Therefore, simply strengthen your mind and keep making constant efforts in times of endurance, however ordinary they may be. "

-From Postscript

THE LAWS OF HOPE
THE PATH TO YOUR DREAM, SUCCESS, AND MISSION IN LIFE

This book offers various simple tips to find happiness: how to overcome depressed feelings and live happily; how to improve your relationships; how to choose a good life partner; how to achieve your dreams; and how to achieve success in your private life and in your business. By practicing these tips, you can find hope in your future and you, yourself, will be the light to illuminate the world.

For a complete list of books, visit okawabooks.com

THE LAWS OF COURAGE

UNLEASH YOUR TRUE POTENTIAL TO OPEN A PATH FOR THE FUTURE

In a world of competition and conflict, it is easy to lose sight of who we really are and become overwhelmed by what happens around us. In this book, Ryuho Okawa presents a new perspective to discover a way to live your life with confidence and strength. This book can guide you to a new future for yourself and the world.

THE LAWS OF GREAT ENLIGHTENMENT

ALWAYS WALK WITH BUDDHA

In this modern society, we often find ourselves unable to forgive someone and maintain a peaceful mind. However, there are ways to lead a stress-free life and enjoy happiness from within. By understanding the Buddhist concept of "enlightenment," you will gain the power to forgive sins and get to know how to be the master of your own mind.

THE MYSTICAL LAWS

GOING BEYOND THE DIMENSIONAL BOUNDARIES

"I believe that once you have finished reading this book, you will find it impossible to return to your old self, for you have now learned the secrets that run through this world and the other.

When you have learned of what has been hidden, will you feel guilt or will you find courage welling up from within? Whichever you experience, you can be sure that the train of life you are riding will take a completely new track."

-From the Afterword

For a complete list of books, visit okawabooks.com

THE LAWS OF FUTURE
HERALD A NEW EARTH ERA

Fight hard for the sake of the future. You must wish, "I will open up a new future, not only for my own sake, but for God's sake, for Buddha's sake, for the sake of my fellow humans with Buddha nature, for the sake of the future of humankind, and for the sake of the world." The road to victory is open before you.

-From Prologue

[This book is available only in local branches and temples. Please refer to the contact information.]

THE LAWS OF SALVATION
FAITH AND THE FUTURE SOCIETY

Why are religions essential to us?

Why should we believe in them?

What is the goal of Happy Science?

—This book will provide you with the answers to these questions.

[This book is available only in local branches and temples. Please refer to the contact information.]

THE LAWS OF CREATION

"No Drop out of the existing "elite track" and create a new one by yourself. This is the true pleasure of life. Respect the weird and strange, and become an honorable eccentric yourself. Be a wonderful eccentric. Be courageous. Become the flag-bearer of the new civilization. Abandon your fearful heart and take on a challenge!"

-From Afterword

[This book is available only in local branches and temples. Please refer to the contact information.]

For a complete list of books, visit okawabooks.com

A LIFE OF TRIUMPH

UNLEASHING YOUR LIGHT UPON THE WORLD

There is a power within you that can lift your heart from despair to hope, from hardship to happiness, and from defeat to triumph. In this book, Master Okawa explains the key attitudes that will help you continuously tap the everlasting reserves of positivity, courage, and energy that are already a part of you so you can realize your dreams and become a wellspring of happiness.

THE ORIGIN OF LOVE

ON THE BEAUTY OF COMPASSION

Why do people love each other, or hate each other? In this book, spiritual teacher Ryuho Okawa answers this question by referring to the origin of love in relation to the secret of eternal life. When you understand the Truth about love, you will be awakened to the wonder of being given life, and you will be filled with love for those around you.

SECRETS OF EVERLASTING TRUTHS

A NEW PARADIGM FOR LIVING ON EARTH

In this book, Master Okawa shows us an extraordinary array of miracles that are increasing by the day. He reveals the fascinating truth that miracles occur through the help of Heaven and even space-people with whom we Earth-people have shared a very close relationship for millennia. He also shows us a glimpse of the power within knowing the existence of a vaster universe created by God.

For a complete list of books, visit okawabooks.com

LEARNING THE SPIRIT OF THE FOUNDER OF HAPPY SCIENCE UNIVERSITY PART I (OVERVIEW)

WHAT IS ACADEMIC DISCIPLINE BASED ON A RELIGIOUS SPIRIT?

"The subject of this book is not just for the establishment of the university. It reveals an unwavering set of guiding principles that will serve as a "North Star" for those aspiring to live in a new era."

-From Preface

THE NEW IDEA OF A UNIVERSITY

THE GROUNDBREAKING MISSION OF HAPPY SCIENCE UNIVERSITY

In this book, the author and founder of Happy Science University, shares his vision for Happy Science University, a new type of university that has no equivalent anywhere in the world. This book opens new frontiers of academia and that provides clear guidelines for leading the world into a better future.

THE BASIC TEACHINGS OF HAPPY SCIENCE

A HAPPINESS THEORY ON TRUTH AND FAITH

When you finish reading this book, three key words, Truth, Faith and Mission that are indispensable to achieve happiness will be left in your heart, and you are bound to discover yourself filled with the wish to live a life of Truth.

For a complete list of books, visit okawabooks.com

PROSPERITY THINKING

DEVELOPING THE MINDSET FOR ATTRACTING INFINITE RICHES

When you think about wealth, its starting point is to benefit more and more people. Or, put differently, being wealthy is to be appreciated by more and more people. This is the source of wealth.

-From Chapter 2

THE MOMENT OF TRUTH

BECOME A LIVING ANGEL TODAY

This book shows that we are essentially spiritual beings and that our true and lasting happiness is not found within the material world but rather in acts of unconditional and selfless love toward the greater world. These pages reveal God's mind, His mercy, and His hope that many of us will become living angels that shine light onto this world.

SPIRITUAL WORLD 101

A GUIDE TO A SPIRITUALLY HAPPY LIFE

This book is a spiritual guidebook that will answer all your questions about the spiritual world, with illustrations and diagrams explaining about your guardian spirit and the secrets of God and Buddha. By reading this book, you will be able to understand the true meaning of life and find happiness in everyday life.

For a complete list of books, visit okawabooks.com

www.ingramcontent.com/pod-product-compliance
Lightning Source LLC
Chambersburg PA
CBHW021003150626
46549CB00012BA/1032